D1062910

THE MOON ROLLS OUT OF OUR MOUTHS

THE MOON ROLLS OUT OF OUR MOUTHS

DEBORAH COOPER
CANDACE GINSBERG
ANN FLOREEN NIEDRINGHAUS
ELLIE SCHOENFELD
ANNE SIMPSON

Ann Floreen Niedringhaus

To Judy and Jamie —
With appreciation for
nearly forty years of
friendship, support and
fun!
Love, Ann

CALYX PRESS
2005

ACKNOWLEDGMENTS

Coping ... with Alzheimer's Disease (Mayo Clinic)
Difficult Valentines (Fallow Deer Books)
Dust and Fire
Good Courage
North Coast Review
The Roaring Muse
Ruah
Shared Visions (Calyx Press)
North Country Sampler (Calyx Press)

Cover Image:
"The Writing Group at Sara's Table"
Original Screen Print by Joel Cooper
<cooperartpoetry.com>

Book Design:
Cecilia Lieder of Calyx Press

A special thank you to
Pat Daugherty

Printer:
Christie Printing Company
Duluth

ISBN # 0-9772376-0-5
In 2006 ISBN # 978-0-9772376-0-9

Copyright © 2005 Deborah Cooper, Candace Ginsberg, Ann Floreen
Niedringhaus, Ellie Schoenfeld, and Anne Simpson

CONTENTS

After a longish period of discussing and recollecting, none of us could remember exactly when it was we started meeting. '98? '99? Even the organized one in the group doesn't know anymore. For a while we considered this a sign that we should not include anything about the group itself - let the poems be on their own, why should anyone care about us? Obviously, the "tell us a little about yourselves" contingent won out. So here are a couple of things we do remember.

We have always met in restaurants, mostly at At Sara's Table, though we didn't always eat. In the beginning (whenever that was) we were all business - just a beverage and right to the poems. Little by little our polite "How was your month?" turned to genuine conversation. We shared serious and trivial illnesses, small triumphs, deaths, news of partners and children, job hunting and work struggles, wedding and grandchildren, present tentacles of past tragedies, birthdays, publications, rejections, travels, retirement, and all the rest.

Oh, we still found time for the poems and always left with our work covered with notes of emphatic and often completely contradictory suggestions. Our work, separate strands, became intertwined. We learned and borrowed from each other. One member's poem inspired another member's work.

This book honors that weaving by following images and themes across the work of all rather than grouping the poems of each individual. The group developed a life of its own and this book seeks to portray and honor that mysterious whole that makes us a bit more than the sum of our parts. We may not know when it all started but we can tell you that we eat whole dinners now, sometimes even order dessert.

es

THE WRITING GROUP AT SARA'S TABLE

When we arrive,
our arms filled with poems,
you, in the next booth,
might want to move off
to the table in the corner.

At first glance,
it might appear that
there are five of us.
At second glance,
a crowd.

We are the soldiers
sent to war,
the small girl
maimed by a bomb.

We are the rain
waking the memory,
the wind, coaxing the clouds
across the sky,
lifting the white lace
of a curtain.

We are the cat
curled on the bed,
the robin in the yew bush,
God in a tutu,
French-blue lilacs in
an alabaster bowl.

The moon rolls
out of our mouths.
The dead rise up between
the pages in our hands.

dc

HOW TONI MORRISON SAVED ME

I wanted to say I love you wanted
to say what a miracle it all is,
put a seed in the ground
and there's a tomato or a flower
and then these babies
my friends grow inside them
selves get born
and what is that magic
slip two hands together,
your arms around my waist
while I'm chopping vegetables,
want to write about these things
but they're so cliché
then I read Toni Morrison's interview
and she said "Everything is cliché,"
so I stopped worrying about original
thoughts or sins or critics or
sap or the terminally hip or
anything else that puts
the pressure on to not
name the miracles.

es

JESUS RISING

I watched Jesus rise
up the side of the Damiano Center on 4th Street.
Ropes and pulleys hoisted
the fisher of men into the air,
hands outstretched and open.

His face and robes glow
with fresh paint as per Historical Society specs.
He is compelling and benevolent looking
though terribly pale,
elegant in this neighborhood full
of broken glass and boarded up windows.

I watched Jesus rise
and thought about loving everybody
even the seagulls
who are the agreed upon enemy
in this city in spite
of the lilting way they fly
or how their songs complement the waves
drumming the shore.

Right now all of the seagulls of the world
are in the Damiano parking lot,
some sort of miracle of bread,
Jesus smiling. Flecks of shattered glass
glint in the light of the sun.

es

THE YELLOW SKIP-HOP

In the woods, a small bird
asks me to follow him,

skip-hops ahead then stops,
waiting for me to catch up.

Surprise of yellow
when he lifts his wings.

I used to worry that I didn't
know the names of things,

bought every field-guide…
mushrooms and butterflies and trees,
but I always seemed to forget.

Now I just make up my own names.

This bird, after all, doesn't know
what they call him either.

At first I wonder where
he might be taking me,

some secret spot where I'll
receive a message or a sign?

Eventually I realize
we're just hanging out

among the sunswirls and
the purple Nana's-hats.

dc

DURING WAR

The robin appeared one morning at dawn
in the yew bush a foot from our window.
Her nest was wedged between three twigs.

How does she sit so long?

If only she'd leave
so we can see if there's down or chick inside.

There are beaks in the shadow.

Mouths rise up like floodwater
and overflow the brim, reaching out.

When will they fly?

This morning the nest is rent and tipped
with just one neck still craning.

On the ground below lies a tiny leg bone.

Now she's there only briefly.
The small head is quiet.

Then both are gone.

afn

DIAMONDS

In the Amsterdam Diamond Market
the dark-jacketed salesman
holds on the back of his graceful manicured hand
a diamond priced at forty thousand Euros.
The mid-day sun lighting the window behind
blurs his silhouette, turns all eyes
to that icy, dazzling chunk.

In the tall townhouse
overlooking an Amsterdam canal
windows are wrapped in muslin. Dusty rooms
are reached by climbing a steep wooden stairway.
Only if you know where to look can you find
the rolling bookcase that hides
a narrow door. In the annex,

light was so meager
that the SS officer couldn't see
the modest diamond on Mrs. Frank's thin hand.
No, he must have known it would be there
and was prepared to ask for it with authority.
It soon appeared on the plump pink finger
of his adolescent girl friend, its tiny facets
faintly glinting as she displayed it
for her gathered friends.

afn

ANOTHER STORM

An Iraqi family, fleeing toward what they thought would be safety, were fired at by American soldiers. "I saw the heads of my two little girls come off," Lamea Hassan repeated. "My girls...I watched their heads come off their bodies. And my son is dead."

Duluth News Tribune, April 2, 2003

April opens with
another winter storm,
stirring the trees with
a huge, invisible spoon,
spitting ice against
the window glass.

The daffodils
I brought home
from the grocery store,
cheating at 'signs-of-spring'
refuse to bloom...
clenching their buds tight,
like the fists of
an obstinate child.

Behind the television screen
they fight another war.
The skyline of Baghdad shines
like the Emerald City.
It is the images
they do not show
that wake me in the night.

dc

RAIN

Time has passed
but pain has not

drops glide down
as wipers slap
forth and back
back and forth

rhythmic
monotonous
the metronome of
memory takes up the beat

- other days of rain

standing wrapped
with arms entwined
as wind and water
pelted panes
and
lightning flashed

walks
wood scented
in an envelope of mist
muting speech
and binding our hearts.

The week you died -
freezing knives
driving
hour after hour as
soaked
I worked to bank the doors
against the flood.

cg

DULUTH
--after William Stafford's "The Light By the Barn"

The rain on the roof that whispers all night
ceases at dawn when a ship whistle blows.

A ship whistle blows hailing the lights
on the shore and raising the waiting bridge.

The waiting bridge rests, saving its strength
to move up and down amid gulls in flight.

The ship whistles rouse the waiting bridge
and the gulls in flight 'til the fog rolls in --

Then the rain on the roof again.

afn

BETWEEN THE CEILING AND THE MOON

My mother's hand
miscalculates her mouth.
She keeps jabbing the cookie
into her chin.
"Are my teeth in?" she asks,
as if this might be the problem.

Last week she told me
she'd been stuck up
on the ceiling
for the longest time.
Today I hang a string
of tinfoil stars
above her bed.

The circumference of her life
is pulled tighter
with each round of the clock,
like a knot…
like a seed
that will break open
elsewhere.

And still, she asks
each time I walk into her room
"Has the baby come yet?"
and something loosens
in my chest.
My daughter is serene and round
and luminous,
as if she had swallowed the moon.

Now the moon
is following me home…
the new moon,
holding the shadow
of the old…
the old moon, graciously
giving itself up.

dc

LAST DAYS

1)
Leaving the house
to drive south on 35…
she hasn't eaten for three days…
I see that the impatiens
in the garden,
a throng of blossoms
for the last three months,
have all keeled over
in the night.

2)
When I am with her in
my chair beside the bed,
stroking her arm
or singing softly
while she sleeps,
I wonder what it is I'm doing…
if she even knows I'm there.

When I am home,
staring into the open freezer
for five minutes,
reading the same line
of the dumb book over and over,
losing my keys,
I wonder what it is I'm doing…
whether she knows that I'm not there.

3)
When the lights go off
for a moment
then come on again,
I make a note of the time.

4)
This morning
through the window
by the bed,
a line of cormorants
divides the sky.
I bring the feeders in,
release the hummingbirds.
The last phlox left

in the side garden
holds the final monarch
by a string.

5)
One by one, I toss
my favorite stones
into the lake,
each one a plea for her release.
Later, when Cam calls and says
she's eating just a little bit again,
my heart flies up
then drops.

6)
I enter the room.
She opens up her eyes
but doesn't take me in.
My face, a language
she no longer comprehends.

7)
We have our last visit
over and over.
I want to say all
the right things,
as if the perfect word
might make a door.
"Door" I try simply.
"Window?" "Sky?"

dc

FIRST DAYS

1)
In the frozen garden
through a shroud of maple leaves
two red begonias bloom.

2)
Dawdling at the cemetery,
October air, downpour
of falling leaves,
none of us can hold
the baby long enough.

3)
The day after the funeral,
in our own separate cities and houses,
the plane to Cleveland or
the car driving to Peoria,
we all, as if slammed by
the same wave, go under.

4)
I couldn't go often
into the part of me
that held her suffering.
Now it seeps out
into my cells.

I want to burrow back in time
and find her laughing
in the lane
but the way is cluttered.

I bump up against
the wheelchair and the lift,
get caught on the days
she would say nothing
but Hail Marys.

5)
Jimmy calls.
My throat closes
and my words cannot squeak out.

I hear him say "I remember when
my father died you told me...
in those early months
the spirit stays close."

The same words she'd given me
when her dad died.

6)
I don't want to be looking for a sign.
I want it to sneak up on me,
bowl me over.
Unexpected.
Unmistakable.

7)
The first day I don't get a sympathy card
in the mail, I cry, feeling abandoned.
I toss the catalogues into the trash
along with the Target bill,
which I think they are cruel
to have sent me.

I remember my last purchases,
the camisole and panties
she was buried in, under
Nana's velvet dress...
the soft, burgundy slippers.

dc

FIRST GRANDCHILD

With each of the children,
though they'd sprouted
in my depths

then grown to take up
every speck of space,

their small feet tapping
at the bottom
of my heart,

I was stunned to finally find
some tiny stranger
in my arms.

But you, first grandchild,
I recognize at once

as if I'd loved you
in some other place

as if I'd missed you all along.

dc

THE SMILE

Laid in my lap,
this natural cradle
you will soon outgrow,
I'm planting kisses
on the soft soles of these feet
that have never touched ground.

Not even one month old,
you look into my eyes
and your small face suddenly blooms
into the sweetest smile,
remaking the world…

the way I imagined my first communion would be…
fanfare of trumpets…
(before it was only the dry wafer
stuck to the roof of my mouth)

the way I imagined my first kiss…
(never having considered the possibility of braces).

This smile makes up for everything.
It says
"I've waited an eternity to meet you,
 swum across the sea to reach you.
 You belong to me.
 I love you so."

I am undone.
Ah, mystical moment
made for a poem!
Wise smiling-Buddha-boy!

And then you tilt your head
and aim the same amazing smile
at the ceiling fan.

dc

FULL MOON

A friend calls late at night,
"Have you seen the moon?
Don't miss it!"

I rouse you and bundle us up;
we hurry down three narrow flights of stairs,
out of the apartment building
to where the sky expands ...

There she is -
huge and close and white,
a halo burning all around her,
then an aura
shimmering green and red
and another soft white ring
smudging into dark, star-lit sky.

"I've never seen a moon like that!"
I point up and turn your head,
"Isn't it beautiful?
Look there!"

You say
"and there ...(pointing at the street lamp)
and there ...(the stop sign in the parking lot)
and there ..."(the radio tower on the distant hill)
You look down and make circles with your finger
in the air above your feet
"It's everywhere!"

Did I miss it?

as

WAR GAMES

When our son was little
he came home from school,
poured a glass of milk,
grabbed a handful of cookies
and clambered up the stairs to his room.

The door slammed shut
but all afternoon we could hear
skirmishes on the wooden floor
with mouth noises that I couldn't duplicate
(let alone spell)
as he moved toy soldiers about his room.

It didn't matter what color their uniforms were,
whether they were wood or plastic or metal,
big or small.
He was Commander in Chief;
his was the power and the glory.

The most violent battles were engaged
if he got teased on the playground
or ignored by his older brothers
or the teacher made him feel stupid
because he wasn't good at math.

Today in letters two inches tall
the headline screams
INVASION.

A three-pronged thrust,
the newspaper explains:
on the ground,
in the air,
from the sea.

Under the desk,
from the top of the bed,
in front of the window.
BANG, BANG you're dead.

as

23

INSTRUCTIONS TO THE WORLD
FROM THE U.S.A.

Expect your lives to be
wretched and desolate; and exercise
patient suffering, but not enough to ennoble.

Be sure you appear somewhat
damaged, your precise flaw hidden enough
to require research.

If that is not possible,
at least be picturesque, preferably
behind an obscuring fence.

Especially, do not show pretensions
to joy or pride. And if you have hope,
keep it from us.

afn

REGRET

A pristine snowfield.
My ruthless steps last till Spring,
ever expanding.

afn

INTERVIEW WITH GOD

In the dream I am a journalist who has landed an interview with God and God is a wrinkly old man wearing an aqua tutu. He can tell that I am a little surprised by His appearance, says He picked the god as a human male thing to match my upbringing, and the tutu (which I don't remember hearing anything about while growing up) well, He confesses that it has always surprised Him that humans, who have free will and can wear anything they like, don't all just gravitate to ballet clothes. Those lushly colored, diaphanous fabrics which lend themselves to twirling - an activity God suggests we spend more time in - are one of the better things we have ever come up with. We discuss fabric for awhile and then I ask Him if humans are really the most evolved of the species. He has a hearty belly laugh, tells me how much we crack Him up, pulls Himself together and tells me no. Says the raspberries, for example, are light years ahead of us. Think about it - there they are with their berries that perfect shade of red, that pleasing texture, they offer up their sweet sensuous selves to the world. They spread joy, don't argue, have flags, feel patriotic, or go to war. They just share their perfect selves and here God reminds me about the ones who were good enough to plant themselves right by where I park my earth-destroying car. They don't hold this car against me, they know that humans are not smart enough to do anything else. I ask about the sparkly crown which is more like a tiara and He says, yes, that's what it is because *tiara* is such a prettier word than *crown* which implies kingdoms and that bad impulse to go to war whereas a shiny tiara just makes a man feel pretty. God laughs, says He thinks He was a crow in a past life and I think Wait! It's me who thinks this crow thing about themselves to explain my attraction to shiny objects so maybe this is one of those lesson dreams, maybe I'm starting to think of myself as God when I should clearly be trying to emulate a raspberry and when I wake up I eat my new role model for breakfast because I have always heard that you are what you eat.

es

SO THIS IS GRACE

Sitting here
by the kitchen window
in the early dawn
of a February morning,
idly stirring my second cup of coffee,

the heat of the sun
surprises me
and suddenly
I realize how very long
I have been cold.

as

ROCK GARDEN

Sometimes in the morning
you help me dress you,
suddenly remembering how to wear a shirt,
or in the evening
you can recite our bedtime prayers.

Moments of loveliness surprise me
where I least expect them -
like these brilliant bluebells that refuse to grow in my garden
though I water, weed and fertilize.

Here they are by the lake
braving gales,
poking up from crevasses in the rock.

as

LILACS

My grandmother arranged them for her living room
in a white metal bowl with lacy scroll brim,
like a hat turned upside down -
purple on one side,
French blue on the other,
white always in the middle.

Today I pass a hedge like hers on a walk through town.
I smell the sweetness of her welcome
half a block away...

   I am sitting at her breakfast table,
   the sun warm on my back;
   through the glass top I see my legs sticking out from the chair,
   bare toes winking,
   as we eat Melba toast
   with unsalted butter and marmalade.
   She stirs her coffee,
   I sip weak tea.

   I hide myself in the cupboard below her stairs
   while she counts 1..2...3

   I try on her big straw hats,
   clomp over cold tile floors
   in her pink satin mules
   with a pouf on the toe ...

My stubborn walking shoes try to stop.
They want to turn into that yard
and sit for awhile in the fragrance.

I imagine knocking at the door.
"Excuse me," I'd say.
"Could I have one -
just one branch of each color?

Please,
could you take me home?"

as

29

GOODWILL

Seated on the couch
I became chilled -
felt a shadow pass over my grave.

That night, in bed,
your father slept
as the first warm rush of loss burst forth.

"It is over," I thought,
sponging red splatters
off the stool, walls, and floor -
leaving carnelian tear tracks everywhere.

Hour after hour,
days on end,
the bleeding continued.

On Yom Kippur my labor began...

Curled up in a ball
on the cold hard floor
I lay alone
all night long
as wave after wave of
unbearable pain
swelled through me
- easing at last with the dawn.

As a show of concern
a friend's new wife
(at her husband's behest)
took me shopping
then to lunch, to distract me.

First, shoes.
  "I buy the cheapest ones for my son."
Then, lawn furniture.
  "Only the best."
Finally, lunch.

"Those little sounds
you make,
you must be having contractions."

Busying herself with salad,
she eyed my plate and said,
"You sure eat the fattest
foods you can find,
don't you?"

Meal over,
she pulled her brown
leather billfold
from her back jeans pocket,
paid up, and
duty done,
dropped me off.

Later, at the Goodwill store,
I felt you tug and
looking down
watched the silvery white
blanket that
nourished you
slip effortlessly out.

Time shifted -
became measured
beat upon beat
by the pounding of a pulse
inside my head.

Head turned,
I gazed at a dirty sink
and leaking faucet
hearing,
as from a distance,
a heavy pounding fist
on the hollow bathroom door.

Not knowing
what to do,
torn between your needs
and theirs,
I reached up
pressed the silver handle down
and watched
as your life
and mine
were flushed
down the toilet.

cg

RIVER DREAMS

Through the darkest season,
dreams of the river carry us.

Current of memory…
the teahouse skirts
the rapids.

The sky, along that
far side of the year,
holding the light.

Shadows of white pine reach
the evening's edge…
fragrance of cedar trees.

Nothing unbidden falls
upon our ears,
just this…

intricate ecstasy
of water,
pure, uncomplicated
glee of birds.

dc

FOREVER

I run my fingers through forever.
I feel the silk of it, the way it moves
fluid like a river.
I can tell that it's perfectly safe.
It is as graceful as that waltz
I always meant to dance, as graceful
as two bodies feeling each other's breath.
Forever is a series of random moments,
a glance of true recognition
or the way a hand
can tenderly touch a cheek.
When I touch your hair
it feels like forever.
Forever is breathing in
the sweet of hyacinths
and the summer promise
of peonies and lavender and thyme.
It's breathing out the aroma
of decaying leaves,
the knowledge of the pure ice
and quiet snow to come.
Forever is the softest sort of summer rain
where my soulmate,
who has finally bothered to show up,
takes my hand
and we go for a walk.
I run my fingers through forever
and it is damp and mossy
with tiny wildflowers here and there
and there like here you can miss them
if you don't look closely enough.
Forever is that sand that slips through my fingers,
that the water pulls suddenly from the shore
and sweeps away down the wild wild river of itself.

es

NIGHT WATCH

Lightly sleeping
within my berth
yet ever aware
of each lift and
heave of hull
beneath me
- the creaking
of seams stressed
to their max
- of lines pulled
wetly taut
with all the
strength a
being could find
to bend
and bind
the wind
within the kite hard sails.

Blood and heart
beat with the
pulse of storm.

Ding ding
Ding ding
Ding ding
Ding ding
- eight bells
and my rest is done.

I rise soundlessly
to replace the
weary souls above.

Moving with care
to spare those
still dreaming,
I brace myself
against walls
and bulkheads -
donning stiff clothes
with one hand.

I am up,
up on deck
under a black
star studded sky.
The wind and spray
strike my face
to brace me awake
and thrill me alive.

I take the helm
bridle-like
- feel the pull
of the sloop
beneath my feet
as she drives hard
as a race horse
across the streaming
foam topped waves.

The clean smells
of cold seas
and freshening breezes
assault my senses
and clear all dreams
from my mind.

This is my watch
 - the night watch.

cg

EARLY WINTER

The woods are turning yellow.
No flickers yet of red-flamed maple
but already the late rains have come,
heavy rains
that weight the leaves till they despair of holding on

if winds,
shifting to the north,
blow hard enough
to extinguish
the spark that autumn barely lit.

I walk quickly past our large front window,
shy to watch the woods disrobe,
as children are afraid to see
a parent's liveliness blown out
too soon

because we forget the beauty
of the naked trees
until they stand proud before us,
their brilliant gifts strewn about,
nourishing the embers.

as

THIS STEP

Somewhere
around the middle of your life

you understand that
it is not the destination.

Nor is it what is waiting
where the road turns next.

It is the step that you are taking now,
or maybe what has stopped you.

It is this soft light, sifting
through the leaves,

the red-winged blackbird
calling from the mountain ash.

It is the secret whispered
in this breeze…
this breath.

dc

CLOUDS

The red clouds line the sky like stretch marks
around the crescent moon navel. And that umbilical cord
which we cannot see and upon which we must depend,
stretches out to the source
which is about to give birth, is always about to give birth
is always giving birth to something, coming for someone else,
that sliver of a navel moon, smiling.

We walked along the ice on the edge of the Lake,
pools of open water everywhere, cracking under our feet.
We joked about it taking us but it didn't.
We were headed for the ice caves and we almost made it.
It was the open water separating us
from that destination, we stood and looked to that place
where we could not go and on our way back
the water did not swallow us either.
It was dark by the time we got back to the car.
The fire we built later, one of the warmest.

That was all before.
Before that other ice cracked
before that other water swept you into its current.
I watched your eyes go under and through
that canal, watched you be born into that other world
watched you go to the other side of that open water without me,
that open water that separates us now.
I always hear those waves
lapping against the shore.
I try to build a fire but it never keeps me warm.

Those red clouds keep coming back,
deep and vivid for that short time
where everything changes,
that time which belongs to them.
Those midwife clouds bleed across the sky
while the universe gives birth
to whatever it will.

es

UNEXPECTED WONDER

I can imagine how it started: unexpected wonder followed by the desire to preserve it. A meteorologist before weather satellites, my father photographed clouds. Everyone told him he was lucky to have "a good job" during the Depression, but he craved a Divine Call. Climbing up on the airport roof to pull in weather balloons, he brought along his camera and tripod. Soon he and my mother were there on the weekends when conditions were right for specific formations. He captured a perfect solitary cumulonimbus set in a pre-storm sky. That image became the trademark for a marshmallow company. His picture of flat nimbostratus, gray and knobby, showed an example so average it appeared in <u>Encyclopedia</u> <u>Americana</u> as visual definition of "cloud". But the rarest form he recorded was a nameless twisted wisp lying parallel to the horizon. Apparently unremarkable, it showed the inner workings of cloud building. Preserved only on our parsonage wall, whenever Dad explained it, we marveled.

afn

LIFE FORMS

I

Dry-eyed cirrus clouds
clasp the stratosphere:
sheer brittle ice wisps that disappear
while they slide past the sun.

II

Cumulonimbus clouds
glide proudly in their channels:
large ships pushed by a master wind.
When one unfurls
into an anvil thunderhead,
hurls down its rain -- that cloud
lives on through the night,
hiding the moon, delaying the day.

III

Cumulostratus cloud blankets
hug the earth, sometimes so closely
they are torn by hilltops. Serviceable
and plain, they simply give up their rain.

afn

TO EVERY SEASON

She left him years ago,
her mind too fragile to sustain health;
yet her stubborn body
and her valiant spirit
cling to life

as winter clings,
with icy fingers,
to the north side of tree trunks
and gasps arctic air
deep into April.

He wishes it would end.
He wants the long good-bye
to finally be over.
He would like to pick up his life again,
to feel young and light and free.

But, wrapped in winter lethargy,
he is as afraid of change
as he is eager for it.

He knows her death will come
as spring comes to the north country,
always sudden
it seems,

though we have been waiting endless weeks
to pack away our heavy sweaters,
to throw open windows
and clear debris from the yard.

She gives him hints,
curling into herself
like buds of deep blue scilla and purple crocus
poking tentatively through the dirty snow.

as

LOVE POEM

I wait for you like the six year old I was
in the train station, numb
from frigid metal, dank cement,
certain the train would leave without us;
running ahead,
bolting from parents' plodding pace,
    deliberate as Clydesdales',
running ahead, but always
running back to prod you on,
knowing I can't
leave without you.

afn

THE LAST NIGHT/ORION'S BELT

Child asleep
in our bed,
I lean my face against
the glass
staring
in the dark...

Three bright stars,
silver knots in the finest
climbing rope to heaven,
stand out in the warm black sky.

"It is time," a voice whispers.
And then, the phone rings -
"Come now, the end is near."

So, with one last glance
through the bedroom window
at the invisible thread

We speed with leaden hearts
to your side
to watch and hold
and finally
let go
as your breath stops...

And there, in the night sky
the strand shimmers,
comes alive in your hands,
as you begin
your easy
swinging
upward climb.

cg

"HE DIED AT 1:45"

"Everything feels like chaos!"
one voice cries out.

Eyes closed,
I silently scream,
"No!
Listen.
Watch, and be quiet."

As I travel the
night dark path
you run
with your new
clear vision.

I, stumbling,
nearly lost in the dark
groping my way
sensing your rapid movements
ahead of me -

leaving me
far behind
on a road I cannot yet travel…

And you are gone.

cg

CANDLE

Your sister
(at the last moment)
announces the absolute need
for a candle.

So, the gift from co-workers
is snatched arbitrarily
from the mantle
and carried along
to the place
we have chosen
for the last farewells.

Carefully our son and I
lay out the prayer shawl
on the oak table
at the front of the stage.

Sparkling gems
of colored glass
are spread
across the cloth
to catch the light.

Finally,
the candle is placed
"just so".

It's light flickers
gently and dimly
in response to the words
of those
who thought they knew
you.

Their words,
spoken quickly,
sink into the silence.

The service over
the people gone
the candle still burning
on the mantle
long into the night.

I sit
alone
in the dark -
remembering
the light in your eyes.

cg

ALL SAINTS

For weeks now,
the light will keep leaving us.

As if in compensation for the sun,
I light a dozen candles.

I rearrange the faces on the piano,
trace a finger down my father's cheek,

which is covered with dust,
making me feel like a negligent daughter.

I still hear his voice in the odd dream
and from the mouths of my brothers.

I wipe his face with my sleeve…
his face, stuck in the same expression
day after day.

Nana's jaw must ache with smiling
after all these years.
Grandad, forever looking off to the side.

One by one,
the faces in these photographs
become the faces of the dead…
my secret saints.

I light a candle
for each one of them,
as if the piano were an altar,

play my Nana's favorite hymn…

flames quickening
with each chord.

dc

WHAT WE KNOW

The figures who surround us
rarely step into the intersecting beams
of our headlights -- but we know they are near.
The space they inhabit is illumined only

by distant stars -- but we know they are near
when their fingertips brush our shoulder blades,
their breath riffles our hair. If we turn around quickly
their shadows withdraw just before we see them.

The path we walk rarely leaves our bright zone.
We keep to huddles tight as fists, think
that those outside are the exiles. But in truth
we are the ones whose cells

silently unknit until we end our days
transparent as the sheerest lace. And those voices
we hear from the darkness have a certainty
stronger than we have ever known.

afn

THINGS I DIDN'T KNOW I'D MISS

The way his hair
those last few years,
precisely Bryl-cremed
through my childhood,
sprang from his head
like a flock of startled gulls.

Watching from the window,
before the wandering began,
when he could still find
his way around the pond,
circling for hours if
we didn't bring him in…
the day I realized he had put on
mother's lilac coat,
her white angora gloves.

The day, wanting to help
as I made lunch,
he set the table, using all the
family photographs as plates.
Ham-on-rye on his
Canadian Air Force face.

dc

BEHIND EACH WINDOW

They land back
in their beds,
the gauze of dreams
falling away,

here and there,
a strand, still tangled
in a woman's hair,
or wound around the fingers
of a small boy's hand.

The mind,
in those first upright moments,
returning to the jungle
or the stranger's face,
then losing hold,

fastening itself back,
putting the water on for tea.
These mugs that will not be
turned into birds,
thrilling the hand,

the table that keeps its shape;
the house across the lane,
set in the same gray
puzzle of stones
as every other day.

Soon, the first door will open.
The first person will come
around the corner,
the way he always does,

briefcase and lunch sack
in the hands
that have lost the memory
of the reins,

the feel of the sweat
on the muscled neck
of the black horse.

dc

CLEANING OUT THE FILES

I am cleaning out my files.
My cousin tells me she is doing the same
and my college roommate,
whose ability to thrive in creative chaos
I have envied for forty years,
has bought a book on avoiding household clutter.
Focus on the kitchen sink, she reads -
that is the whole secret.

We each know others who are doing this, too.
A tsunami of the would-be organized
about to engulf Office Max and Staples
sweeping the shelves of color-coded labels and folders,
software, paper clips and pens.

This is not the annual after-tax,
before-garden spring cleaning.
This is a sea-change,
a desperate attempt in time of war
to prepare for death or defeat it,
though the idea that we can do either
is preposterous
and we all know it.

Still we try to clear our minds
and somehow to unclutter our souls
as they were in the beginning
when our planet was neatly woven together,
flung across the universe
and it was Good.

as

QUAKER MEETING

I have come to Quaker Meeting because I like the idea of sitting quietly in a circle with people who are contemplating spiritual and non-violent ways, to become centered and serene but I notice that it isn't really quiet - there is traffic outside, people are downstairs having coffee - I would like some coffee - and others walk across the impossibly loud floorboards, they shift positions in creaking pews and I think about how Quakers always remind me a little of oatmeal and now I am thinking about oatmeal and of my suspicion that most truly good people eat oatmeal because it is so healthy and cheap and wholesome and I have tried to like it but stubbornly continue to hate hot cereal of all kinds indicating that I'm probably not very good deep down inside and, as if to prove it, my mind wanders into that territory where you are never supposed to go when you are in church and though the Quakers are likely more open-minded than the Lutherans on this topic I'll bet they would say that Meeting isn't the place to be thinking about sex so, of course, it's all I can think about and not the sweetly loving spiritually connected kind, no, I'm thinking about the fishnet-stockings-talk-dirty-fuck-me-now kind of sex, the very worst kind to be thinking about in church, the kind that gets you sent to hell in short order and the only other thought that enters my mind is that there are clearly some problems with my personality which reminds me about yesterday when I was talking with a friend whose very existence I was celebrating at his birthday party when he told me "Go ahead and have the cheesecake because you are at the point in your life where, if you ever do date again, it will be because someone is interested in your personality." hmmmm...my personality...very bad news...and here, in this quiet peace-loving circle, it occurs to me that I could put out a hit on him, take out a contract on his life, these things are probably done all the time, and though I have lived my life committed to pacifist ideals and he is a long-time friend who has a young child, this murder for hire seems the only reasonable response and then I start to wonder about group rates because it's just like they say about that slippery slope, once you consider having one person killed it's not much of a leap to start killing off others like the man who asked me when the baby was due when I was not pregnant - yes, he will have to go - and I suspect the Quakers aren't as big on hell as the Lutherans but they may have an emergency one for people who think about lewd sex and develop hit lists during Meeting so I try hard to think of something, anything else but am so spiritually small and shallow that I remember more people, more slights and insults and wonder if I should add them to the list but soon I find my bloodlust waning and I congratulate myself on this spiritual progress, this new-found lack of homicidal impulse and I almost laugh out loud but pull myself together enough not to and try to pay attention to the thoughtful and uplifting messages some of the others are moved to share but my back and neck are starting to hurt, I have to go to the bathroom, want to shift positions but am afraid of the thunderous pew creaking drawing attention to my degenerate self and finally it's over and someone good and glowing with pure and peaceful thoughts is inviting me downstairs but I don't go there.

es

HOSPITALITY

The woman behind the desk in Admitting
wears a wide black strap around her neck
to hold her ID card -
in bold white letters it proclaims
GOD IS AWESOME.

It is lunch time and
she is alone in the small office at the hospital.
"What are you doing here?"
She glares as I step to the door.

"I have an appointment..."
"Where are your doctors orders?"
"I don't have any..."
"WHAT!? No orders?"
"It's the routine mammogram my doctor recommended."

She pushes her chair back
as if I were a leper,
swivels to her file cabinet
and reaches in.
"Where were you born?"

She shoves a clipboard across the desk.
"Fill out both forms. Sign in three places,"
then picks up the telephone.
"Your patient is here without orders!!"
she scolds my doctor's office.

She wears a wide red band on her wrist
that quivers as she slams down the phone
but I can read the bold white letters:
WHAT WOULD JESUS DO?

as

56

KNIVES

Nasty people
know just where to plant the knife.

So sly,
they wait and smile
listening and observing
for anything you care about.

Then,
with surgical precision,
they slip the blade
right through your ribs
to your heartfelt love
or your object of pride
and single it out…

exposing it as small
and cheap
with an uplifted brow
and pitying look.

cg

CONGRUENCE

To you
who are now leaving
the cluttered dinner table
my words are as arrows
piercing your warm flesh
- releasing the blood warm feelings
you hide carefully within.

Your fingers pressed to the tiny wounds,
you try with shallow conversation
to stem the flow
that would reveal to all present
your inner being
writhing with discomfort
at any show of emotion
or sign of weakness.

Wine is drunk.
Dessert is offered.
Children discussed.
And grief…

denied.

cg

MINNESOTA MARCH

The fog hangs in the air
like dusty curtains.

A sluggish rain
makes pockmarks
in the crusty snow.

I open windows
for the sound of it

but it is drowned by
a cacophony of crows,
angry as candidates.

At Cub, I space out
all the things I've come for,
toilet paper, milk and bread

and fill my cart with
daffodils instead…
four dozen miniature suns,

pay through the nose
to have the taste
of blueberries

break open
on my tongue.

dc

Stare. It is the way to educate your eye.
quote from Walker Evans

I

Against Spring's shadows
neon blue ice at lake's edge:
radiant crescent.

II

You hold out your hand.
From your palm shimmering peaks
rise, surrounding us.

III

Crescent moon rises --
an alabaster bowl piled
with transparent pudding.

IV

Hanging there, solid,
the icicle claims briefly
the moving water.

V

From the deep peephole
in my door -- a distorted
hall and the next door.

afn

ONE NIGHT STAND

This poem is a one night stand.
This poem sauntered through the ethers,
flirted with me and made me laugh
until I took it home to my room.
It seemed like such a good idea at the time.
This poem is the next morning.
That awful moment when I know
it was a horrible mistake, that poem
on the pillow looking at me
expecting something more - coffee? Breakfast?
And then the poem says just the right thing,
sighs with a complicated mixture
of melancholy and contentment.
I realize I could develop feelings for this poem.
What can I do? That poem
is staring at me, requires some sort of words.
It won't let me, for once,
just keep my mouth shut.
This is the biggest problem with poems -
they are demanding, they always expect
more and more words.

es

AT THE QUAKER MEETING

At the Quaker meeting
I've been meaning to get to
for at least three years,
I am trying not to think
of Ellie's poem,
the one in which,
at the Quaker meeting,
she can't stop thinking
about sex.

This isn't easy.
I was the child,
standing in line
for the confessional,
thinking impure thoughts…
the most embarrassing of sins.

I am trying to be absolutely still
but I am fidgety
because the inner voice
of my stomach
is growling loudly.
I'm sure that all the Friends
can hear.
Next time I'll eat
before I come.

Well into the long silence,
the Friends continue to come in,
as quietly as they can
in winter boots.
I am surprised that Quakers
are stragglers.
In Catholic church,
if you arrive beyond a certain
crucial point,
the Mass cannot be counted.

I hear a sound
I first interpret
as a rush of wings
and think that this must be
a sacred moment.

Praying I am not being called upon
to deliver some message,
I try to hear it as the furnace.

But then, one of the Friends
is moved to speak.
"Truck-truck-truck!"
bleats out the little voice behind me.

dc

THE BREW

Head tilted back
the glass lifted
high
a communion host
or blood of Christ
"Take this in
and you will be changed."

The foam spills
over the amber
leaving white flecks
upon your lips.

Eyes close,
neck muscles
slide up
then down,
and lines resolve
as the brew
slips down
easing all pain,
opening the door
to easy conversation
...the confession
of sin.

cg

COUNSELOR

The phone rings
and there is that warm voice
on the other end of the line.
"How are you?"
you ask.

The question is sincere.
The silence awaits
a thoughtful answer.
No rush.
No agenda.
No sense of duty done.

Painful topics lift up
to humor,
peak at reverie,
and ebb back to pain
with fluid ease.

And with each change
the tension diminishes,
the wave of pain subsides,
until at last
there is only a
calm and gentle sea.

cg

MAGIC FISHES

As embryos
we start out with gills
that eventually disappear until
poof! We have lungs.
We are magic fishes
and to this day my dreams
are filled with water,
huge waves engulfing everything.

My ribs hurt
when I breathe.
All that work to rise and fall.
They remember the time before air.
They remember water
sliding over gills -
languid, effortless.

es

ANATOMY OF ALZHEIMER'S

Your hands are fish fins,
rotating fans,
butterflies...
they flit, flop, circle away from your body.

You watch them
detached
to see
if they can grasp words out of the air,
catch a memory and
fondle it for you,

lift you into the sky
or release you
from this earth
into some deep warm sea
where you are swimming.

as

HORIZON

The horizon stretches
out ahead of me
as barren
as flat
as grey
as the future without you.

The dark clouds
scudding overhead
add weight to this portent
of dread and sadness.

Why no silver lining,
no streams of sunlight,
or vibrant rainbows?
The signs of promise are absent.

The tinder of hope can now
be found only within -
on a landscape unseen,
uncharted and unexplored -
where many a weary soul
is lost.

cg

A YEAR AFTER
THE DEATH

Pacing my kitchen
late at night,
as agitated
and aimless as
a late season fly,

I see again
the ice skim
breaking away from
the coast where
it was anchored,

floating out
from the shore.
Buffeted by
choppy waves
in the bay,

it rides them
with a flat, brittle
grace as it
disappears
around the far point.

afn

SPRING EQUINOX

Winter's long nights drove us inward,
downward,
to sit with questions...

quiet enfolded us
til sometimes
answers sputtered like candles.

Now our eyes are used to the dark
and it is hard
to welcome the longer days;

we wear solitude
like a thick wool sweater,
afraid to fold it away for the season.

But ice cracks,
doors open to a noisy world
and rivers gush through,

tumbling
like a grade school class at recess -
ready or not!

as

SPRING POEM

Robins skitter across the snow.
They cover the tree branches
and peer into my window,
their famous red breasts
a carpet for Spring.
The pigeons have started cooing in the eaves.
Crows sit together close on the wires
which criss-cross the neighborhood
and those squirrels
have a definite frolic in their tails.
My yard is full of lovers.
The forsythia buds swell on the bushes
ready to burst, they fill the hillside
with the idea of yellow.
Promises pop, spill, swirl everywhere;
they get in my eyes, tangle themselves in my hair,
they tumble down the hill
and land at my feet.

es

SECRET

The earth lends itself to me,
lets me run my fingers through it
so I can feel
what I will eventually become.
It whispers to me "Enjoy."

The earth loans a bit of itself
so I can plant raspberries, allots a corner
for my sustenance of blueberries,
lovingly allows for
the red erotic possibility
of strawberries. The strawberries
are wanton and lustful, they take over
as much of the garden as they like
and they like it all.

es

SONG OF CATS AND DIRT

The cats have been slaughtered for the ritual
of quizzing anatomy students.
We will take a hacksaw to their heads,
rip out organs
without a prayer or a song.
We treat the cats like dirt
because we fail to consider
that a teaspoon of dirt
may contain five billion bacteria,
twenty million small, filamentous fungi,
and one million protozoa.
If the bacteria who live
in our intestinal tracts
abandoned us,
we'd be lost.
We are nothing
without the commune of creatures
who inhabit our bodies.
The mitochondria who joined up
with every single cell -
we owe them our lives.
Somewhere we know this.
We can remember,
breathe deep and quiet enough
to hear the songs
of our mitochondria,
pick up a handful of dirt
and embrace our cousins.
Every moment of our lives
could be a joyful
family reunion.
In a better world
to treat someone like dirt
would be the highest of honors.

es

THE HUMAN

In lush woods
I scratch away the surface,
mosses, leaves, vines,
to see the color.

In Ohaingu, sand was off-white,
the hew of sun-bleached
wood, old straw,
radiating back African sunshine.

Ruacana, a day's travel away,
was warm burnt orange
primeval clay, glowing,
an echo of the lingering sunset.

A friend told me about
pure black Hawaiian
volcanic ash where
white stones can write graffiti.

Maybe this soil
can be uncovered too.
So I dig, determined
to make my mark.

afn

CHINA

Now the trees have become birds
molting their feathers on their flight in
down into the essence of their roots
of the earth of themselves of what sustains them
into the dark regenerative spaces
they drop their feathers
in this dance with the hawks and the eagles
who ride and tilt on the currents of air
that pull them South, we are all in flight
South and inward to China
and maybe that's where they all go
the way we thought when we were kids
digging a hole to the other side
of the earth, to the land of all things
exotic and mysterious, we keep digging our way
inward to our own China, over our own great walls
where all of us can hear that sound
of one hand clapping of one feather falling and falling
always falling inward and South falling
always falling to China.

es

WINTER STORM WARNING

The sky is packed with
sack-of-flour clouds.
I know that I should go now
in the nick-of-time
to Super One
with all the wise Duluthians
stocking up

but this mauve afghan,
the one that Nana knit,
has pinned me to the couch.
Later, craving stew,
eating the last two crackers in the box,
I will, along with all the other slackers,
call Dominoes
and tip big.

dc

BOB

This cold has been around for a long time. It has settled into my lungs, has made itself at home there. As far as I can tell, it plans to stay for the rest of my natural life no matter how much garlic or lemon juice I consume. At first I am annoyed but, being adaptable, I get used to the idea. I name the virus Bob. Maybe it won't be so bad having a roommate again because sometimes people who live alone for too long become peculiar, even strange. Perhaps Bob was sent to save me from taking too great an interest in acquiring a houseful of cats. It's not so quiet around here now - even my neighbor remarks that he hears me coughing in the night right through the walls of our houses. I simply laugh and say "Oh, that was just Bob." I try to get used to Bob's quirks and preferences but it's tiring to have him around all of the time, it's not long before we start fighting. I say "If you're going to live here you're going to have to wash a dish now and then and I'm getting pretty sick of being the only one who ever cleans the toilet!" Bob says nothing, just makes me cough - he's monotonous that way, can't really carry his part of the conversation. Sometimes I loathe Bob and I sense that he loathes me, as well. I tell him "Go already if you don't like me anymore!" But he never does.

es

THE BIRTHDAY BALLOON

Your birthday was two months ago.
The balloon that hugged the ceiling in your den
is losing energy and
showing its age;

it drifts around the rooms,
rising and falling with daily currents,
so anywhere you go -

when you try to find the bathroom
or sit at the kitchen table
or settle into your chair to take a nap -

you bump into "Happy 70,"
a gaudy red and gold reminder
that time has gone too quickly.

I try to remember
when you were half this age
and you could navigate your life without a compass,
when your eyes had light behind them
and your smile was confident.

I try to remember
what you were like
before your mind was pricked by disease,
before life began to leak from your body
and leave you flat.

Then I imagine that your spirit has escaped,
and seeped into the walls,
that it hovers in these rooms
and follows me
though I cannot see it.

Sometimes it surprises me
with a presence on my shoulder
or a gentle nudge
that makes me turn
and catch you
smiling at me,
plump and bright with recognition.

as

HER HANDS

The last year, her hands
curled into knots,

the hands that brought the music
to my childhood,

Chopin floating up the stairway
while I fell asleep.

It was work at the end,
opening her hands

to wash them and massage
the lotion in

then fasten on the sheepskin-covered splints
to keep her fingernails from digging through
the pale, fragile skin of her palms.

Holding her hand meant wrapping yours
around a tight bundle of bones.

How is it then, that in
this photograph,

taken the day she saw the baby
the first time

the hand she lays upon his head
is the soft, curved wing of a bird?

dc

MOTHERHOOD

I was
never confident
I could calm you.

Each time
you started
I wondered
if you
would
cry forever.

But I digress.

In a few minutes
I will call you.

I will hear
your firm voice.

We will
make our plans.

I know
the kind of day
it will be:

I will
work hard
to be
a good listener,

not
give advice
or criticize,

and I will
hold back
the grateful tears.

afn

MARY'S VISION

Tentatively he asks,
"Have you thought about God?"

"Maybe..." she whispers
with a suspicion of a smile
as she turns toward the wall,
"maybe not enough..."

He reaches out to her.
She clutches her son's hand
as if she could hold on to him forever,
as if she could watch him grow old,

as if she had time to read
all the books that neatly line her shelves
or outlive the cat curled
in the bedclothes at her feet.

All those years ago
when he planned to spend
his summer earnings on a car
she insisted he put some aside for school,
she told him the first girl he brought home
was not suitable at all,
she always encouraged his vocation...

in so many things,
he admitted now,
she was right.

She liked to be right!
But today he needs to tell her she is wrong
when, churning and delirious with morphine,
she cries out
"Look!
There is a beautiful place ...
and they won't let me in."

as

83

FRIENDSHIP

A place to be real.

I shared my heart,
bared my soul,
listened to all your pain,
rejoiced in your growth,
encouraged your dreams…

and you said,
"You were my project."

cg

BAD ADVICE

"Ask for what you need,"
the counselor sagely advises.

"I'm afraid," I respond.

"What are you afraid of?
The worst that can happen
is that they will say no."

That is not the worst.
The worst happens
when they say, "yes."

They suck you in -
make you feel special,
cared for
and valued.

Then the recriminations begin:
"You drain me."
"You hurt."
"You are to blame."
"Everyone dances around you."

Don't ask -
give.

Give
till there's nothing left.

What does a counselor know?

cg

FEAR OF VALENTINES

Children know. Even three year olds
feel the visceral power of doilies
and construction paper,
the authority of pastel stickers.

I've opened valentines,
drawn in by the hearts,
found myself looking for clues
in lace and ornate writing
to what the offering means,
what I must give in return.

Confronting a valentine
adults need that yellow tape
used at crime scenes --
yellow tape that plainly says,
"stand clear", "danger",
as it flutters in the wind.

afn

WARNINGS

Avoid contact with skin
the label warns
(in the world's smallest print)
flush with water
in the event…

Grasping the tube
in my left hand
I squint at arm's
length with
widened eyes
at the message
too late.

The fingers
of my right hand
are transformed
webbed
a mythic creature
half duck
half human

I stand now on one limb
and survey
the muck about me
with equanimity,
unmoved,
glued to the spot.

cg

MARRIAGE

I

There is the official story.
Even we
have admired its shiny,
impenetrable veneer.

II

I remember the day
I first decided
not to guard
myself against you.

III

We have endured
grief storms
that blew us
to our separate
wailing walls. With time
and seeing the world
we've learned
the small scale
of our suffering. But
there is no size to pain.

IV

I was taught
I should pour myself
into you. But you
don't want to be
force fed like grass,
drenched
with fertilizer -- don't
want to end the season
congested and sluggish,
unnaturally green
from my ministrations.

V

Our argument, abandoned,
remains there, as if we've
thrown a tablecloth over
an already set table.

IV

We do not
tend a garden plot
carefully planned --
no black plastic
to block weed seeds,
just soil
open to the sky.

afn

THE DANCERS

With the first turn
of that first dance
sixty years ago,
they turned into one of those couples
that does everything together.

Now they are forgetting
together.
She loses words.
He loses keys and wallets
and his way.

"The armadillo has five red blooms,"
she beams. He calls the police,
certain he's had his pocket picked again.
Then later, when she finds the wallet
safe upon the closet shelf,
he blames the cleaning crew.

"I can never get this phone to work,"
she shouts. He rushes in to save her,
patiently punching the buttons
on the remote, holding it to his ear.
"Must be the battery."

And yet, each time the music starts,
they tango or they samba
or they jitterbug.
They never miss a beat.

dc

LATELY I'VE BEEN LOSING JEWELRY

First it was my father's wedding ring, and then
it was just one earring of the pair I'd given

my mother, chosen because they shimmered
and dangled -- moved as she moved. I don't know

how long they need to be gone before I decide
they are permanently lost. Till then I have to

fight my urge to hunt for them constantly. I wish
I were part of a tradition that taught me the ring

was taken for my father to wear in another world,
that my mother has her favorite earring right now --

but I believe our stories seep into our bones from
the moment of our birth; and to borrow another's

tale is like donning a prosthesis after amputation --
you can walk on it, but your blood
does not flow through it.

afn

HERE I STAND

Recently
when we weren't looking,
a door slammed shut
on the cluttered room behind us.

Strewn across the floor
were all our lasts
just as we stepped out of them,
not knowing

there would be no more trips
or walks in the woods,
no concerts or parties or plays,
no full night's sleep ...

Now I stand naked
in a stark white room
my firsts hanging neatly at the other end,
a long cold walk away.

as

ROOMS AND FURNITURE

"We have only the present moment",
someone says again.
Again, I disagree.

The moment that
I open up her hands,
curled now into tight fists,
rub lavender lotion
into her thin skin,
a drawer unlocks in me…

and we are playing
our sonata,
my fingers on the high part
never quite catching up
to her hands,
two perfect dancers
on the piano keys.

Rocking my daughter's baby boy,
I slip through a door
into the made-up song
I sang when I rocked her.
Same scent of baby skin.
Just down the hall,
my father's whistle
joins me.

We are filled with rooms
and furniture and hallways,

trapdoors
and windows, looking out
into the distance up ahead.

Sitting here,
on my end of the couch,
writing

and watching you
between the lines,

sitting there,
on your end of the couch,
reading,

that window opens
where I know
someday
one of us will be gone.

A teeter-totter tips, as if
one kid's jumped off.

I stop the poem
and lean toward you,

lift the book
out of your hands.

dc

IF I WERE THE MOON

If I were the moon
I would turn your tide.
You would draw maps of me,
would want to learn everything
about my topography,
you would lick me to see
if I am made of green cheese or not.
You would memorize the names
of my mountains and seas.
If I were the moon
you would watch for me.
You would study my face and my curves
and the way my movements
make shadow pictures on your walls.
If I were the moon
you would smile at me
and I would climb in through your window.
I would fill your room
with my own particular madness inducing
lunacy producing light.
I would shine on you and make you howl
until I could taste my name
on your lips and in your mouth.

es

FAR AWAY

across the dark arc
of the sky

I want to think
you're thinking of me,

sitting in your favorite chair,
an open book, forgotten
in your hands.

I want to think your hands
are wanting me,
my skin imagining your touch,

my eyes remembering
your eyes,
looking at me.

Somewhere along the line
that spans the distance
in between us

my thoughts of you will find
your thoughts of me

and bloom in the night
like a new star
beneath this half-a-moon,

this moon I want to think
you might be looking at
right now

outside the window
by your chair,

thinking of me, across the dark
arc of the sky,
writing this poem for you.

dc

The Writing Group At Sara's Table

Candace Ginsberg   Deborah Cooper   Anne Simpson   Ann Niedringhaus   Ellie Schoenfeld

INDEX OF POEMS BY AUTHOR